Années de Pèlerinage

COMPLETE

Franz Liszt

DOVER PUBLICATIONS, INC., *New York*

Published in Canada by General Publishing Company, Ltd.,
30 Lesmill Road, Don Mills, Toronto, Ontario.
Published in the United Kingdom by Constable and Company,
Ltd., 10 Orange Street, London WC2H 7EG.

This Dover edition, first published in 1988, contains all the
music from *F. List / Godï stranstviĭ dli͡a fortepiano* (F. Liszt /
Années de pèlerinage [literally, the Russian is "Years of Wander-
ings" rather than "Years of Pilgrimage"] for Piano) as published
by Muzgiz, Moscow, in 1952 (edited by Ĭa[kov] I[saakovič]
Mil'šteĭn). In the present edition: the editor's preface and the
footnotes appear in a new English translation (for further details
see the Note to the Dover Edition); the original errata are
corrected directly in the musical text; a new detailed English table
of contents has been prepared; the three illustrations and the
editor's commentary have been omitted; and Russian translations
of the Italian tempo indications have been deleted from the music
pages.
The publisher is grateful to Mr. Vladimir Leyetchkiss for
making his copy of the music available for reproduction.

Manufactured in the United States of America
Dover Publications, Inc., 31 East 2nd Street, Mineola, N.Y.
11501

Library of Congress Cataloging-in-Publication Data

Liszt, Franz, 1811–1886.
   [Piano music. Selections]
   Années de pèlerinage.

   For piano.
   Reprint. Originally published: Moscow : Muzgiz, 1952.
   Contents: Années de pèlerinage. Première année : Suisse =
First year : Switzerland ; Deuxième année : Italie = Second
year : Italy ; Venezia e Napoli = Venice and Naples : supplement
to the second year ; Troisième année = Third year—[etc.]

   1. Piano music. I. Liszt, Franz, 1811–1886. Années de
pèlerinage, lère–3e année. 1988.   II. Title.
M22.L77A56   1988   88-751411
ISBN 0-486-25627-8

Dennis E. Burbank

Editor's Preface[*]

THE PRESENT VOLUME CONTAINS all the pieces that Liszt included in the cycle *Années de pèlerinage* and published in definitive form between 1855 and 1883. The musical text of these pieces has been freshly checked against the original editions published during the composer's lifetime and the complete works edition [*F. Liszt: Musikalische Werke, 1907–1936*]; in those cases where it proved necessary, the text has also been collated with other editions. In clarifying and commenting upon the text, use was also made of a number of Liszt's autograph manuscripts, particularly the hitherto unknown manuscript of the *Première année*.

The editor's goal has been to collect from various sources the composer's directions and remarks on the performance of the pieces comprising the cycle. Therefore, in editing the text, attention has been paid not only to the composer's indications found in the latest editions but also to the notations he made in the manuscripts and earlier editions, as well as those instructions, additions and corrections with regard to performance that Liszt recommended to his pupils in his last years.

To avoid confusing the observations and variants established by the composer in the definitive version of the pieces with his earlier observations, variants and instructions, the latter have either been distinguished by their smaller size (when they have been introduced into the text) or have been placed in footnotes or the commentary.

Thus the composer's text of the last edition within his lifetime has been completely preserved in this edition and has been printed, with the inclusion of all remarks on performance, in the regular text size. All the additions that have been assembled appear in a smaller size. Those additions which are undoubtedly the work of Liszt himself are printed without any substantial reservations (such remarks are merely placed in parentheses in certain cases to make them more distinct). Those additions for which it is still not fully proved that they go back to Liszt, as well as those made by the editor for elucidation of the composer's instructions contained in the text, are enclosed throughout in square brackets.

The composer's orthography, not always sufficiently precise and correct from the viewpoint of the established norms of notation but on the other hand very personal, artistically precise and raising no doubts as to execution, has been retained without substantial changes from considerations of principle; it has merely been subjected to the most indispensable editorial emendation. Obvious small misprints and slips of the pen have been corrected in the text without special explanations. General performance instructions, the history of the composition of the entire cycle, information about the individual pieces and their programmatic content are given (alongside textual notes) in the commentaries. In the same place will be found information about the precise meaning of a number of musical terms used by Liszt.

In the supplement to this volume are printed: (a) "Lyon," the first piece of the original version of the cycle; (b) *Apparitions*, a short cycle very close in its conception to the *Album d'un voyageur;* (c) *Tre sonetti del Petrarca* (in their original version); and (d) *Venezia e Napoli* (in its original version).

J. Milstein (Ia. Mil'stein)

Moscow, 1952

[*]This is a complete literal translation of the Russian preface; for differences in the Dover edition, see the next page.

Note to the Dover Edition, 1988

IN THE PRESENT EDITION, which is directed toward performers, students and general readers rather than musicologists, the very extensive editor's commentary of the 1952 Russian edition has not been translated in extenso. On the other hand, some use has been made of it in the translation of the footnotes on the music pages. In the Russian edition, these footnotes were of two main types: some of them appeared as complete statements right on the page (all the footnotes of this type have been translated), but most of them merely stated (in Russian) "see commentary." In the case of the latter type of footnote, whenever it was possible to extract the gist of the corresponding section of the commentary a new English footnote has been created as a free abridged paraphrase; this type of footnote appears here in square brackets (where only a part of a footnote is a paraphrase of commentary material, only that part is in square brackets). The extracts chosen all involve practical considerations of the musical text or execution. No material was taken from the commentary when the sections referred to in the footnotes involved notated variants of a musical passage, explanations in Russian of Italian-language indications in the music, long technical discussions of specific readings, information on the title or genesis of a piece and similar matters.

Années de pèlerinage

(Years of Pilgrimage)

Première année: Suisse

Chapelle de Guillaume Tell

*) Throughout, the metronomic tempo indications, which follow the established tradition derived from Liszt's pupils and in many cases preserve the composer's own practice, give only an approximation of the desired speed. [Liszt himself opposed metronomic indications as an imposition upon the freedom of composer and performer alike.]

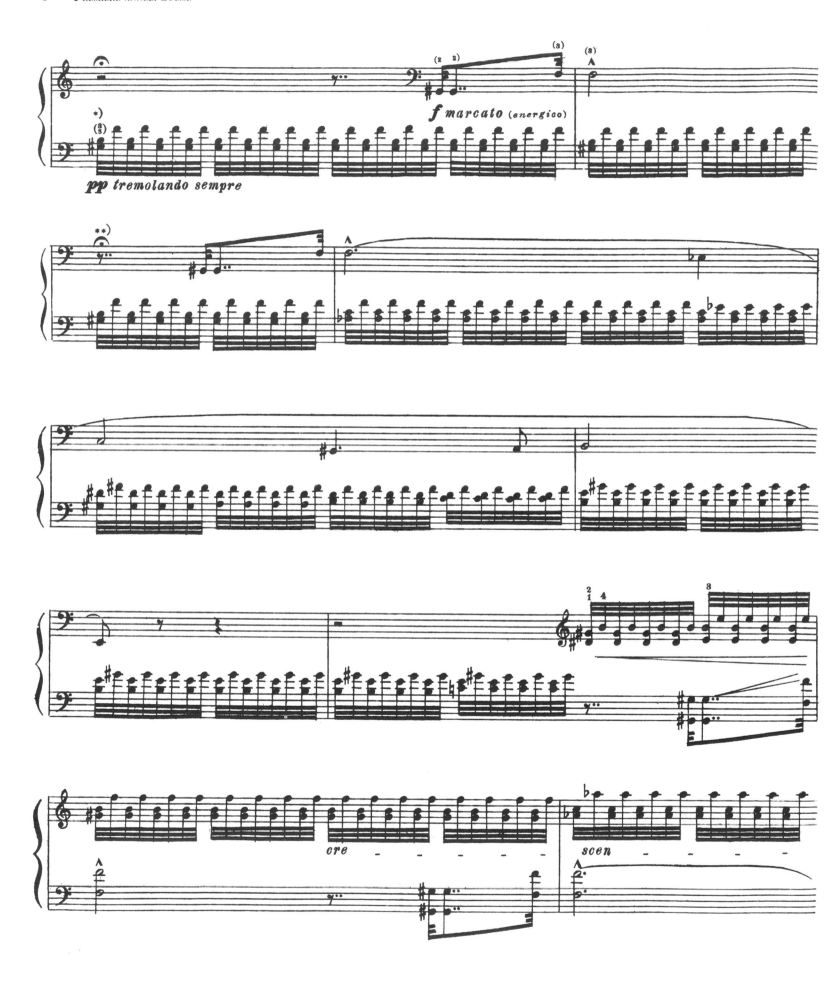

*) The execution of the *tremolando* must correspond to the **prescribed** rhythm (in exact 32nds!).
**) [Klindworth recommended a fermata equivalent to two quarter-notes.]

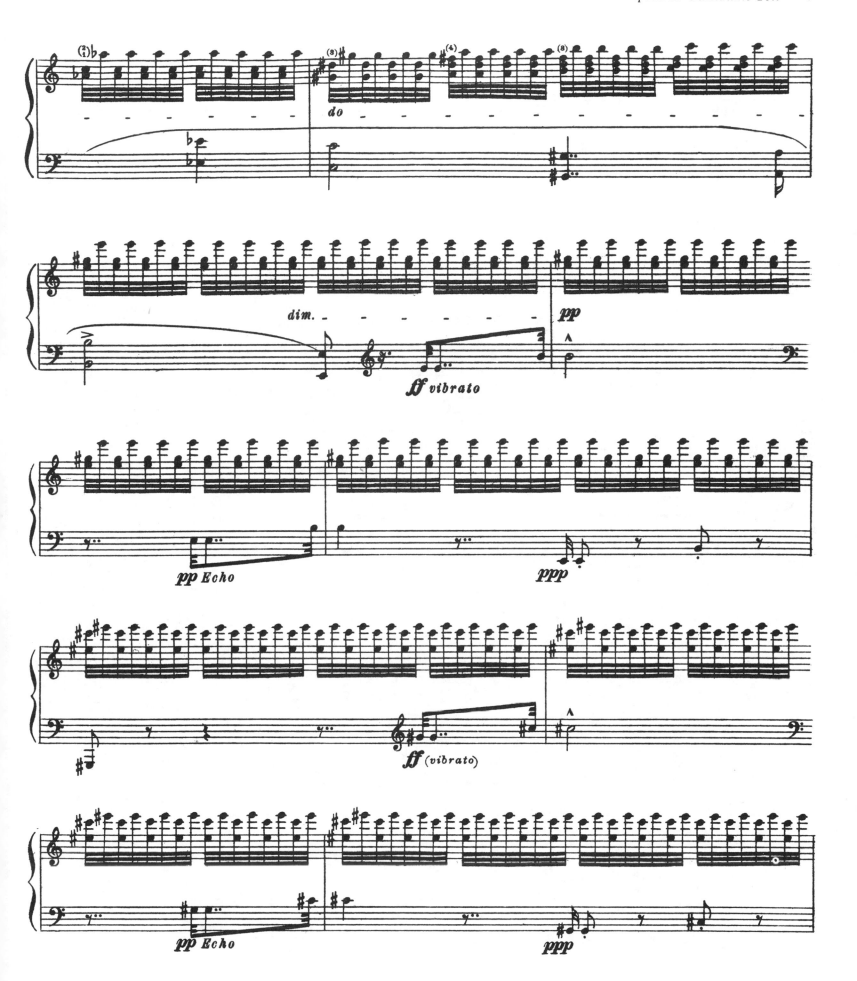

*) The mark ⌃ over a group of notes was an invention of Liszt's to indicate a noticeable strengthening of sonority in the entire group of notes.

Au lac de Wallenstadt

*) This is the fingering indicated by Liszt himself [to pupils, not in editions], doubtless intended for large hands and not suitable for every pianist.

Possible variant fingerings are: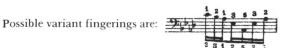

*) The basic text prints the reading of the definitive version as found in the original edition (Schott); the added small reading is that of the first version (see *Album d'un voyageur*), which is the one printed in the complete works edition (*F. Liszt: Musikalische Werke*). Klindworth and others have:

Pastorale

*) [This *ppp* is lacking in the autograph MS.]

Au bord d'une source

*) [The *e leggiero* is added from the autograph MS.]

*) [In the autograph MS, Liszt apparently intended to supply an *ossia* for the last four measures on this page. In the third measure from the end of the page, the original edition has a *b*-natural for the last note in the left hand.]

*) Possible variant fingering:

*) [The *ossia* is in the autograph MS as well as the original edition.]

Orage

*) [Neither the autograph MS nor the original edition indicates what seems to be a necessary pedal release between the two pedal indications.]

*) [Only the autograph MS shows this crescendo.]

*) [In mm. 7–8, 11–12 and 15–16 on this page, the fingering is from the autograph MS; it does not appear in the original edition.]
**) Thus in the original Schott edition and the complete works edition. Klindworth and others [arbitrarily] have:

Meno allegro

stringendo

*) Thus in the original Schott edition and the complete works edition. Klindworth and others [arbitrarily] have:

**) Thus in Schott and complete works. Klindworth and others [arbitrarily] have:

*) [The autograph MS originally had an entire episode after this measure, later deleted by Liszt.]

*)Cadenza ad libitum

marcato

cresc.

*) [Liszt originally intended to print this cadenza in smaller type.]

*) Thus in the autograph MS. In the original Schott edition and the complete works edition the tie between the *f*'s is lacking [probably by oversight].

Vallée d'Obermann

*) [The autograph MS has *con duolo* and *pesante* at the opening of the piece. In measure 5, the MS has the accent on the first note, not the second.]

*) [The dynamics are based on the MS.]

Un poco più di moto ma sempre lento ($\quad$ = 88)

*) [The *pesante* is lacking in the MS. In the 11th measure on the page, the MS ties the high *a* to the following one.]

*) [Klindworth arbitrarily omits the lower *c*-sharp from the chord.]

*) Thus in the original Schott edition and complete works edition. Klindworth and others have:

*) Thus in the MS, original Schott edition and complete works edition. Klindworth and others have:

*) Liszt originally had *Prestissimo* instead of *Presto,* and *furioso* instead of *tempestuoso.*
**) [The text reading purposely preserves that of the MS and original edition.]

*) [The 16th-note is based on the MS; the 8th-note of the original and complete works editions is obviously a misprint.]

*) [Thus in MS. All editions adopt the reading shown in smaller type.]

*) [As in MS; various editions differ.]

Dennis E. Burbank

Églogue

Allegretto con moto

*) [The assertion that these chords should consist of *c* and *g* is unsupported by the MS and the original edition.]

*) [The *p* is restored on the basis of the MS.]

*) [The MS at this point has *raddolcente*.]

*) [In mm. 3 and 5 on this page, the MS has *p*. In m. 14 the MS has *sempre dolce*.]

Le mal du pays

*) [In the first measure on this page, the MS adds: *il canto espressivo assai.* In m. 5, the *rit.* is lacking in the MS. In mm. 7 and 9, in the MS the first 16th-note in the left hand bears an upward quarter-note stem. In m. 14, the MS has *Più lento.* In mm. 20 and 21, in the original edition the top *e*'s are tied.]

Les cloches de Genève: Nocturne

Deuxième année: Italie

Sposalizio

*) This is Liszt's own fingering for mm. 3 and 4; variants have been suggested.

**) Execution: [music]. [The three recommended arpeggio executions on this page derive from Liszt's pupils.]

***) Execution: [music]

****) Execution: [music]

*) Execution:

*) [The version in regular-size type is that of the original and complete works editions; the version in smaller type is given by Klindworth and others.]

*) [In some editions, including the complete works, this chord is *c*-sharp/*e*-natural.]

*) Execution:

Il pensieroso

Canzonetta del Salvator Rosa

*) Translation of song text: "I move frequently from place to place, but I can never change the object of my desire. My burning love will always be the same and I too will always be the same."

*) The version printed smaller occurs in some later editions (Klindworth and others).
**) [Klindworth supplied a variant execution that avoids crossing hands.]

Sonetto 47 del Petrarca

*) [This is Liszt's own meter indication, doubtless implying a double ¾.]

*) This is Liszt's original notation (on four staffs); [Klindworth supplied a two-staff version].

*) [It is essential to maintain this division of the melody between the hands, which is based on weighty considerations of sonority.]

Sonetto 104 del Petrarca

*) This measure is a quarter-beat longer (Liszt often does this in cadenzas, ornaments and similar passages).

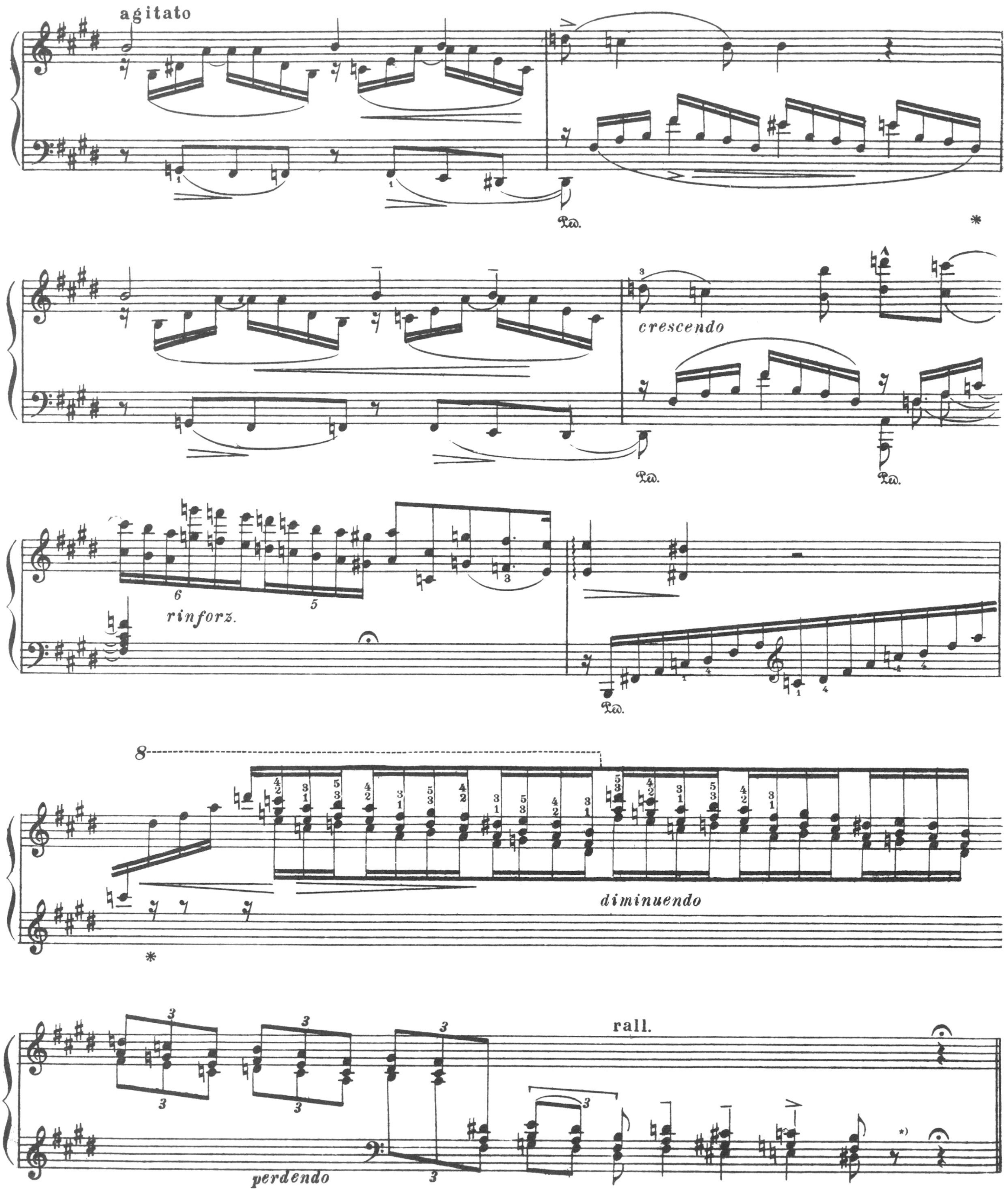

*) [The rests thus in the original and several later editions; in the complete works edition, the eighth-rest is omitted.]

Sonetto 123 del Petrarca

*) [Thus in the original and complete works editions; Klindworth arbitrarily changes the notation.]

*) Thus in the original Schott edition and the complete works edition; Klindworth and others have: ▤ .

*) Thus in the original Schott edition and the complete works edition; Klindworth and others have:

Après une lecture du Dante:
Fantasia quasi sonata

*) This pedal indication (pedal for five measures!) goes back to Liszt himself [apparently to depict the strange noises of the Inferno].
**) [In the original and complete works editions, the next-to-last 16th-chord is *b*-flat/*e*-flat, probably a misprint.]

*) [Thus in original and complete works editions; Klindworth and others omit the *d* from the first four chords in the left hand.]

*) Thus in the original Schott edition and the complete works edition; Klindworth and others have, not without good reasons:

**) The original Schott edition has: Nevertheless, we accept the correction made in the complete works edition on the basis of two copies of the MS corrected by Liszt himself; this correction doubtless corresponds better to Liszt's genuine intentions than the version adopted by Klindworth:

***) Thus in the original Schott edition and the complete works edition. Klindworth has:

*) Thus in the original Schott edition and the complete works edition. Klindworth has:

Tempo I (Andante)

Andante quasi improvisato

Andante [♩=96]

*) [In measure 7, this page, the original edition has a minor chord. In m. 11, the original and complete works editions lack the rest and chord enclosed in broken parentheses; added here in accordance with Klindworth and others by analogy with m. 9.]

*) [The first 4 mm., according to Liszt's instructions, are to be played in a very free recitative manner; we have added the *ossia* line for clarity, following the lead of Klindworth and others; the original and complete works editions merely have: *con 8ʸᵃ ad libitum.* The first 16th-note of m. 14, according to Liszt's instructions, should be played *sforzando.*

*) The mark ∧ over a group of notes was an invention of Liszt's to indicate a noticeable strengthening of sonority in the entire group of notes.

*) Originally Liszt had, in place of the general term *con strepito*, the more picturesque *infernale;* [the change is in line with the more experienced composer's avoidance of colorful instructions].

*) [The flat sign in parentheses is added on the basis of the complete works edition as being more convincing in the harmonic context.]

Andante

*) [The sharp signs in parentheses were added by the Russian editor.]

poco a poco più di moto

*) [The original and complete works editions omit the *d* in the last two chords; Klindworth's emendation is adopted here.]

Andante (Tempo I)

Venezia e Napoli

Gondoliera

*) [The MS has *un poco marcato* under the left-hand part.]

Canzone

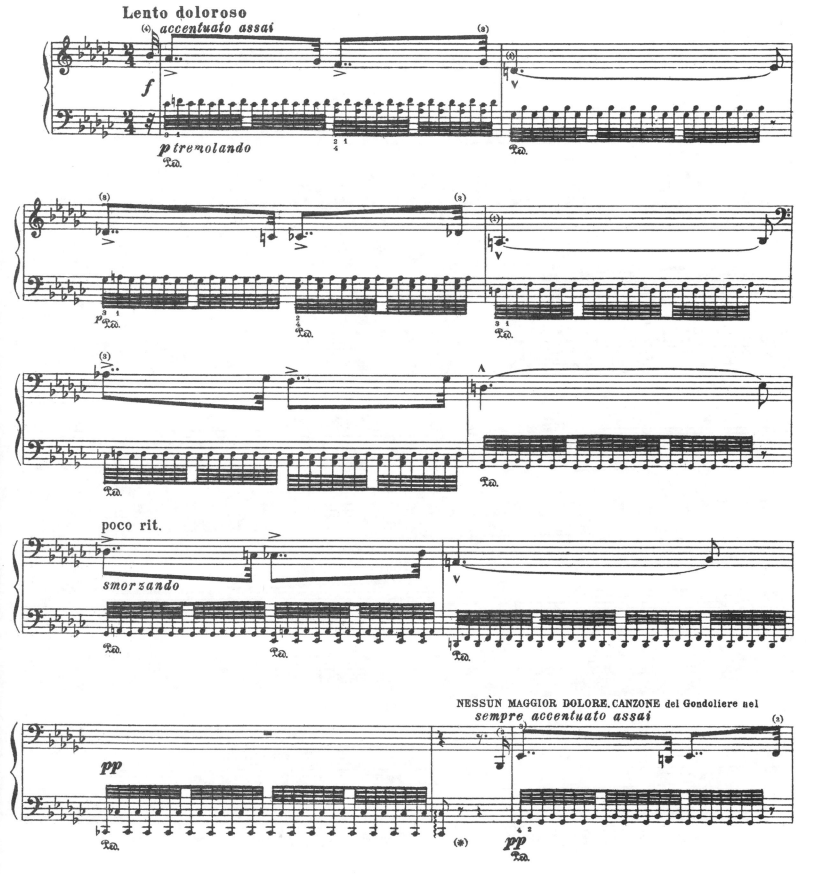

123

„OTELLO" di ROSSINI

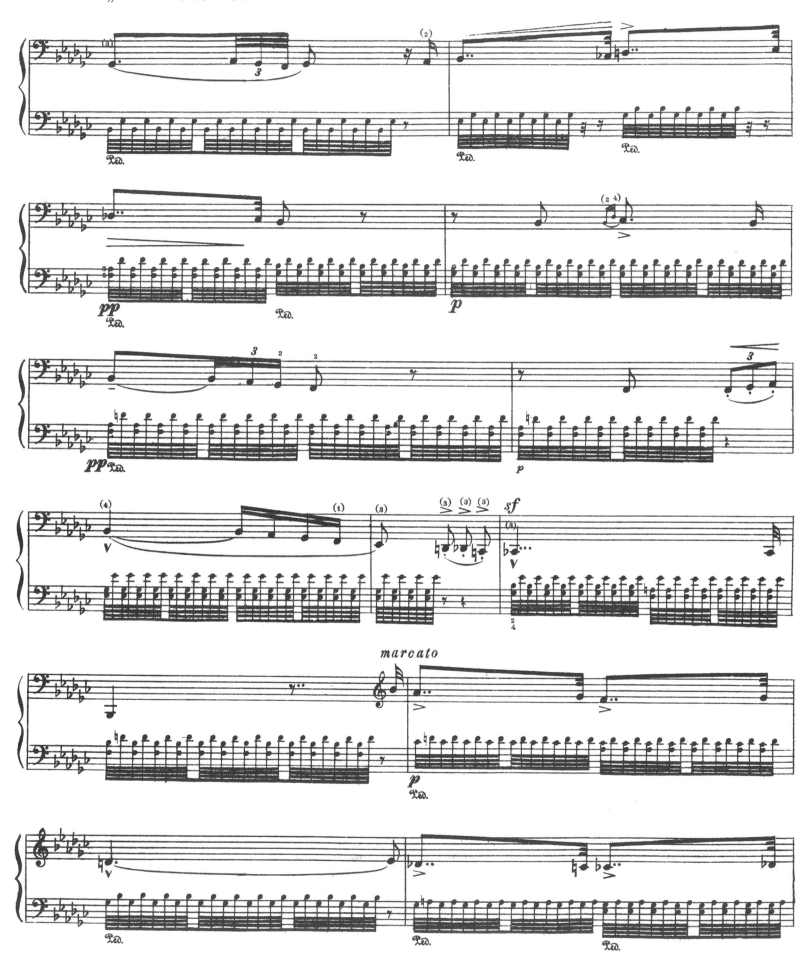

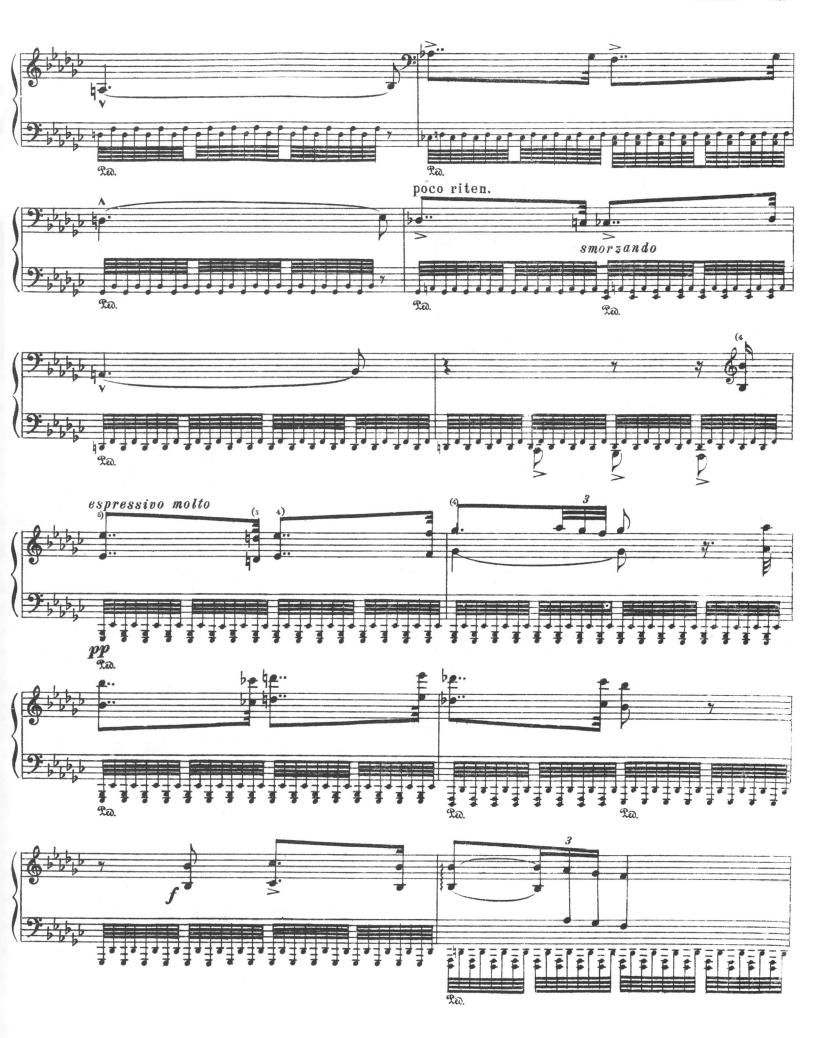

*) [These last 3 mm. occur in one edition from Liszt's lifetime and in the complete works edition.]

Tarantella

*) [The main text shows the reading of the MS, original edition and most later editions; the *ossia*, an emendation from certain later editions, is worth considering.]

CANZONA NAPOLETANA

*) Thus in the original and complete works editions; Klindworth adds a flat-sign in front of the c, without sufficient reasons.

*) The mark ⌃ over a group of notes was an invention of Liszt's to indicate a noticeable strengthening of sonority in the entire group of notes.

Troisième année

Angélus! Prière aux anges gardiens

*) [These are the only 8 mm. in which the harmonium part diverges from the piano part.]

Aux cyprès de la Villa d'Este I: Thrénodie

accelerando

poco a poco crescendo

più agitato

sempre legato

marcato   tremolando   marcato

tremolando

*) [In m. 5, the *c*-sharp appears in the original edition, the complete works and Klindworth; the suggested *e*-sharp is by analogy with m. 1. In m. 17, the main text has the reading of the original, complete works and some other editions; the *ossia* follows Klindworth and others.]

Aux cyprès de la Villa d'Este II: Thrénodie

*) [This first left-hand chord is, mistakenly, *e/e* in the first edition.]

diminuendo
sempre legatissimo
mf
una corda
mf
sempre dolce e legato
crescendo

Les jeux d'eau à la Villa d'Este

un poco più lento

Sunt lacrymae rerum / En mode hongrois

Marche funèbre

Andante, maestoso, funebre

Sursum corda

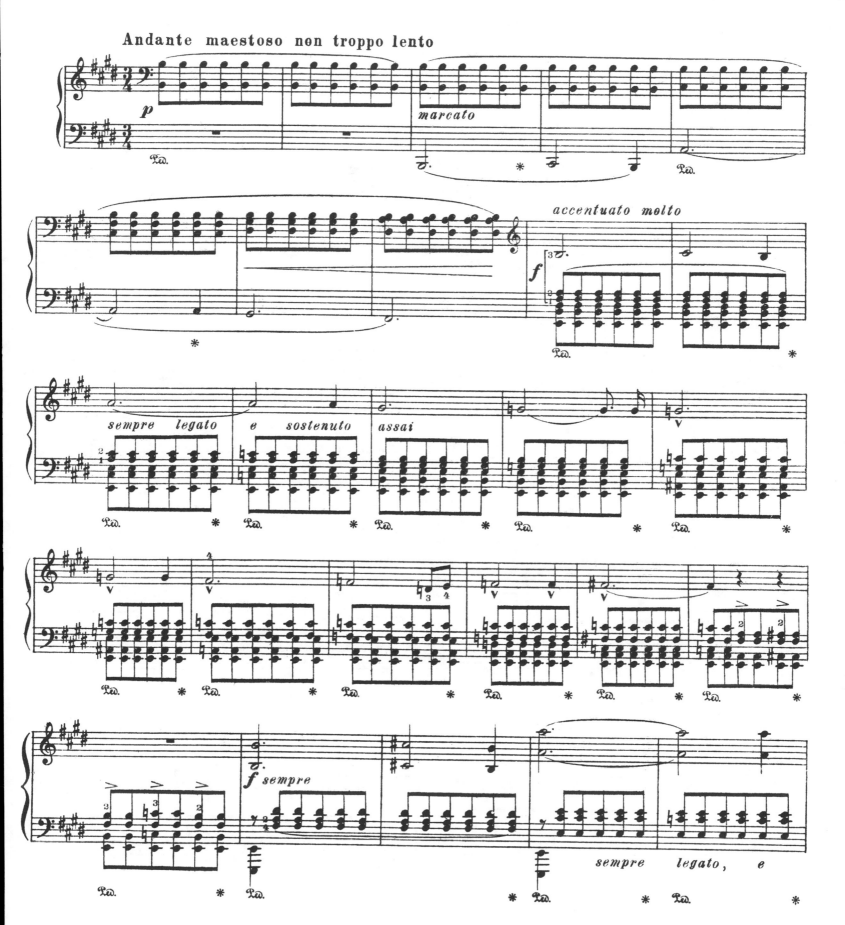

Appendix: Related Works

Lyon

(Vivre en travaillant ou mourir en combattant.) *)

*) ["To live in honest toil or die fighting": the motto of the workers of Lyons.]

**) Double lines ⬚ indicate a crescendo of tempo. Single lines ──── indicate a descrescendo of tempo. The sign ═══ indicates a pause briefer than a fermata. [These were innovations of Liszt's to indicate the nuances of the musical flow.]

*) [The main text retains the reading of the original and complete works editions; the *ossia* suggests an emendation.]

Apparitions

1

2

Fantaisie sur une valse de François Schubert

VALSE DE SCHUBEPT
Moderato

Tre Sonetti del Petrarca [Original Version]

Sonetto 47 di Petrarca

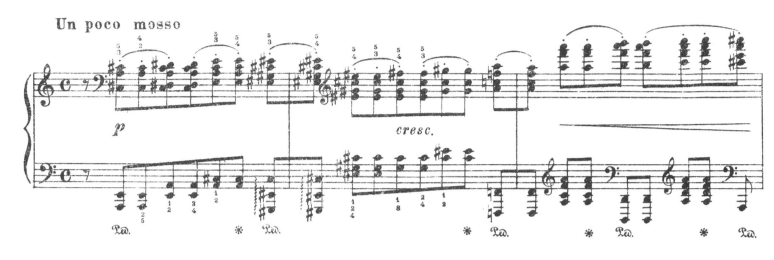

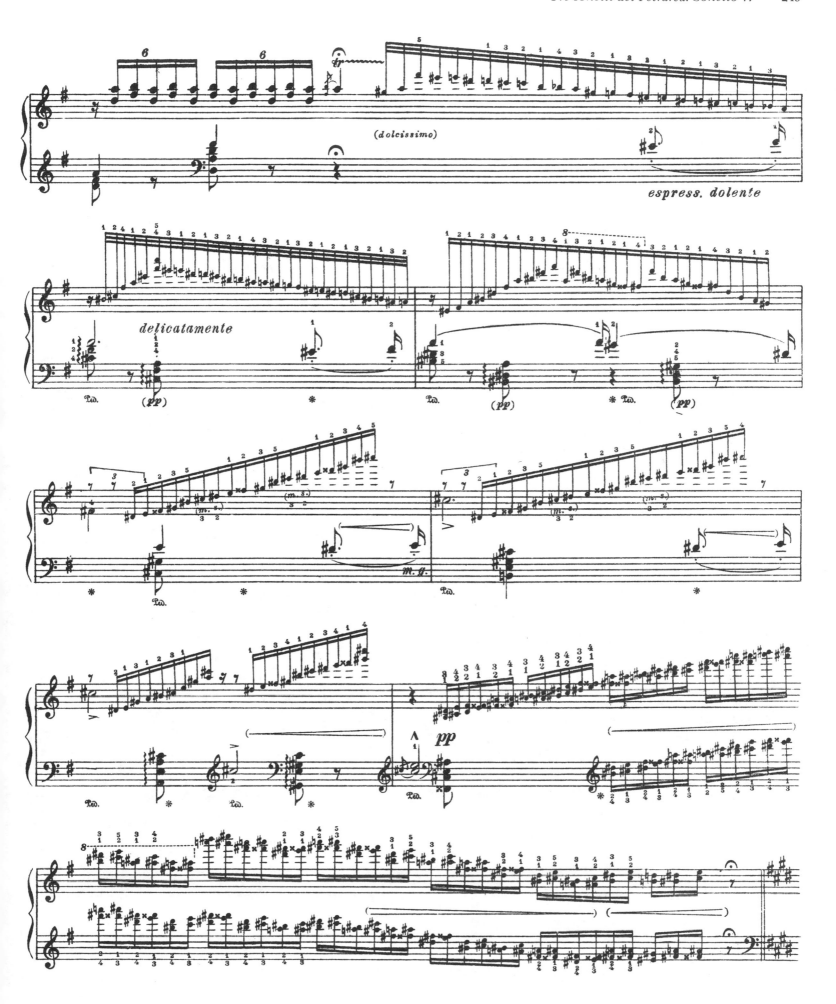

SONETTO 104 DI PETRARCA

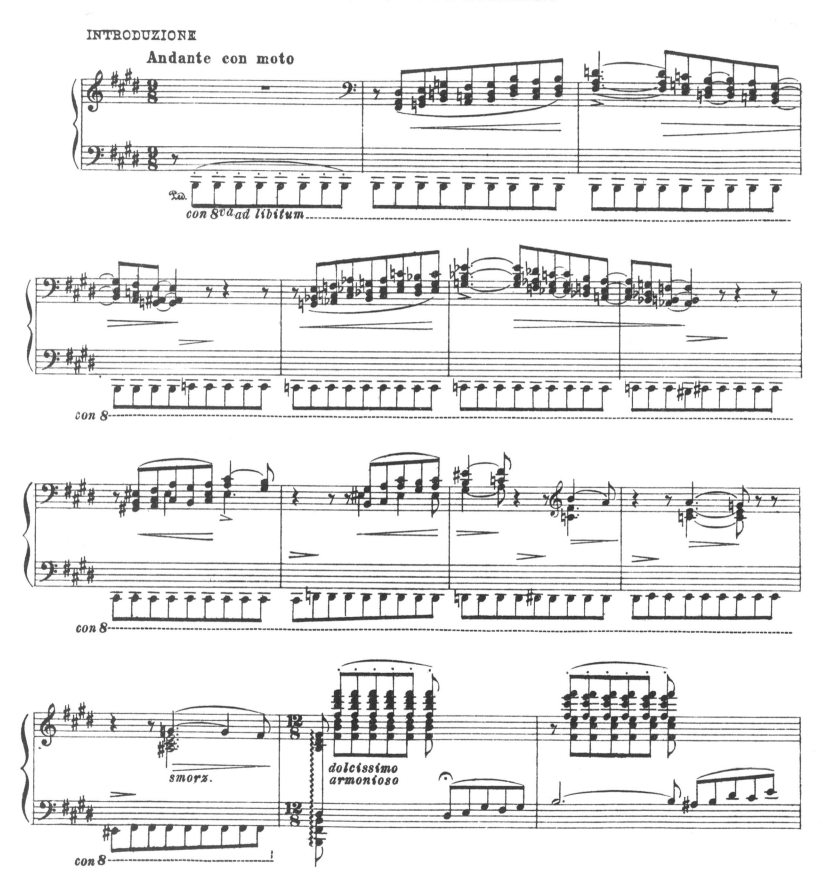

SONETTO 123 DI PETRARCA

Venezia e Napoli [Original Version]

1

Ossia:

Un poco agitato

cresc.

il più f possibile

2

3

dolce armonioso

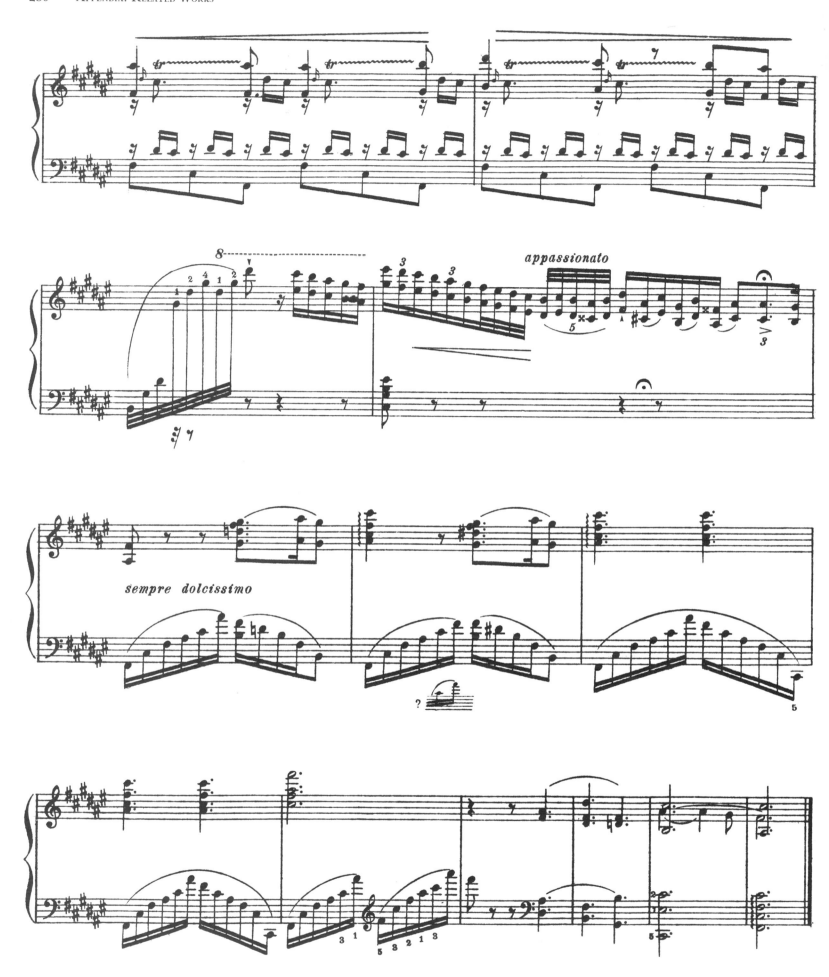